Don't 86 Your Restaurant Sales

Put Butts in the Seats with The ROI Engine

A Turnkey Digital Marketing
Program for Restaurants

Matt Plapp

info@braughlerbooks.com

cover illustration: iStock.com/AdrianHillman

Printed in the United States of America

First printing, 2018

ISBN: 978-1-945091-86-5

Library of Congress Catalog Card Number: 2018951531

Ordering information: Special discounts are available on quantity purchases by bookstores, corporations, associations, and others. For details, contact the publisher at:

sales@braughlerbooks.com
or at 937-58-BOOKS

For questions or comments about this book, please write to:

info@braughlerbooks.com

Braughler™
Books
braughlerbooks.com

Contents

CHAPTER 1

Create Your Own 'Radio Station'

Have you ever wondered what it would it be like if your business had its own radio station? No, not a real radio station. A 'radio station'. For years, I've challenged small business owners and sales professionals to consider this possibility. In my opinion, one of the biggest issues facing businesses is that the audience they 'talk with' on a daily basis isn't nearly as large as it could or should be. Of course, when I say an audience, I mean an audience that knows, likes, and trusts them.

If you look at the ordinary channels of media and marketing that you buy for your business — radio advertising, TV advertising, print advertising, newspaper, magazines, direct mail — they all have an *audience*. And reaching this audience is the key goal of your spending. A radio station has cultivated a listenership that enjoys that station, and so they tune in on a daily basis. A TV station has a following because people watch the shows and appreciate the content they put out. Similarly, a magazine or a newspaper company has an audience that — on a daily, weekly, or monthly basis — opens the pages of that publication for a variety of reasons: to see what's happening, to understand important issues, spark new ideas, learn about trends, get tutorials, and much more.

Your business has the ability to do the same, but in a different way. Let me explain with an example: In Cincinnati, where I'm from, a typical radio station can reach roughly 200,000 people on a weekly basis. That sounds like a big audience, but when you break it down, it's much smaller than what *you* have the ability to reach on your own. Radio stations measure their listenership with what's called Average Quarter Hour, or 'AQH'. This means that for every 15-minute period, they reach a smaller number of people than in their total listenership. So, that 200,000-person radio station is probably reaching, let's just use a round number, 10,000 people every 15 minutes.

Now let's imagine it is *your business* that is spending this money on radio ads. In the entire city, there are about 10,000 people who might hear your $200 commercial. And if you take those 10,000 people and narrow them down to the people who are actually listening, you're probably clos-

	# CURRENT FANS	GOAL
Facebook		
Instagram		
Email		
Other		

er to 5,000 folks. That's because people get distracted — by their kids, by their iPhone, by a traffic-light, by their thoughts, by their surroundings, or by another radio station altogether. So, of the 10,000 you thought would be listening to your commercial, only about 5,000, in fact, are. Of those 5,000 people, how many live in the area where your business is located? Let's say you own a single-location business in Northern Kentucky, in a town across the river from Cincinnati. Well, that just knocked off another 90% (maybe even closer to 95%) of those 5,000 people. By my estimate, you're now reaching only 500 people. And lastly, if you eliminate those listeners who are not in the market for what you sell, or know your brand well enough to recognize or care about it, you're getting closer to 100 people. In short, you just spent $200 to talk to 100 people.

Now consider what you might be able to accomplish using recourses you already have. Resources like: a Facebook page, a Facebook personal profile, a YouTube channel, an Instagram account, Pinterest, email-marketing, text-messaging, Messenger. These are existing routes you can use to engage an audience that *knows*, *likes*, and *trusts* you. I can positively promise you that *ANY* small business or professional salesperson reading this book has the ability to cultivate and create an audience larger than 100 people through those channels. Oh, I left out LinkedIn. If you add that to the mix, you've got, in essence, an additional 'Facebook' business page with 1,000 fans. Think about all this. You've got a personal Facebook account with 500 friends. You've got a LinkedIn account with 1000

CREATE YOUR OWN
RADIO STATION

MONTHLY - FWD
500 + NEW CUSTOMERS

MONTH 6
3.000 +

MONTH 12
6.000 +
NOW YOU
HAVE HUGE
AUDIENCE

www.restaurantmarketingroi.net

connections. You've got Instagram with, say, 200 followers. You've got an email list of 1,000. You've got a text list of another 200. Plus, you've got a Messenger subscriber following of an additional 200 potential customers. (If you don't, this book will cover how you can set that up.) Thinking conservatively, you've just now surpassed — by a factor of 10 — what you can purchase on the radio station in your town!

So that is what I mean when I say you can create your own 'radio station'. As a small business, as a large business, or as a professional salesperson, you currently have the ability to reach a larger audience than your advertising dollars could possibly net for you. The caveat is you have to do the hard work to harness those people into one 'place'. And you have to plan to reach them systematically.

In this book, we're not only going to talk about how restaurants can create their own *radio station* but also how they can create a monthly marketing plan to reach out to those people in that radio station, and drive them into the restaurant, in a predictable manner, with trackable offerings. So join me, won't you? Let's go ahead and get started. Let's go ahead and turn the page...

Visit the link below to register your book and start the online tutorials
www.roiengines.com/p/welcome

CHAPTER 2

Channels You Can Use to Create Your 'Station'

Now that you understand the concept of creating your own radio station, and the power of it, let's do a deeper dive into the various channels you can use to get the results you want and deserve. As you might guess, there are a lot of options out there. We've already covered some of the more obvious ones that you are probably using already: Facebook, LinkedIn, email marketing, etc. And then there are some fairly obvious ones that you're probably not using: YouTube, Facebook Live, texting, Facebook Messenger, Instagram, and Pinterest. And a couple you might be using, but aren't taking full advantage of. Of those, I'm specifically thinking of your website and your in-house marketing.

When it comes to a website, most businesses have the typical "click here" to give us your email address/join our newsletter/give us your cell number/join our email list/etc. form of customer harassment.

Guess what? Nobody wants to join your email list. Nobody wants to join your newsletter. However, people do want to join a *program*, whether it be a VIP-Offers Program, a Rewards Program, an imaginative Customer-Incentives Program, or something similar. So, before you go asking for any email addresses, examine your website and ask yourself if you are framing your offerings in a way that *REWARDS* your clientele, or *ATTACKS* your clientele. The difference can be profound when it comes to your bottom-line.

Visit the link below to check hear about ALL of the options
www.roiengines.com/p/channels

Now let's talk about the in-house experience. Typically, when you go into a restaurant, you see the table-toppers on the tables, you see the posters in the bathroom, you see that card the server gives you when you pay your check, and then some. I've got a picture of a restaurant (on the right) that I visited recently. At meal's end, they presented me with

my check and a really attractive card, which they put in the tines of a fork. When I opened the card, there was a space for me to enter my email address. Well, I've got a few problems with this approach: ONE: most people just aren't going to take the time to write their email address. TWO: they might, like me, have terrible handwriting, so no one will be able to read the email address. And THREE: an employee would need to transcribe all those email addresses into a spreadsheet before uploading them into an email program.

How could this be done differently? I want you to consider how such info could be gathered digitally. We could start with some old technology, like QR Codes, which has some legs, but a lot of people don't have a QR Code reader on their phone. But some-

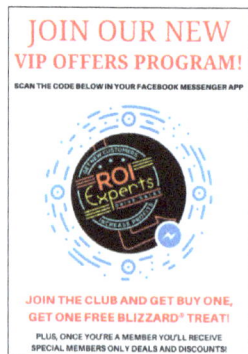

thing people do have on their phones is access to the internet; they can quickly and easily go to a website. And, more than likely, they have Facebook Messenger, and Facebook Messenger has a *messenger code* option.

In my opinion, this will only get bigger as the months go on, but as for now, a lot of consumers don't know that they have the messenger code option. Take a moment to check out the tutorial guide; the link below will take you to a site that will show you how you can use (Facebook) Messenger (and a related URL) to get people signed into this program automatically, eliminate the typos, eliminate having to transcribe the data into a spreadsheet, and eliminate the wasted manpower. You'll also find 10 Tips to help you attract the attention of these people and get them to act more often versus: "Give me your email address." Believe it or not, I actually had the following experience in a restaurant, recently. When I went to the register, the cashier said to me, and I quote, "You don't want to give me your email address, do you?" Needless to say, I replied "no".

Visit the link below…or better yet scan the code to check out how to use the Messenger Scan Code

www.roiengines.com/p/scancode

Sometimes, the channels that you use to grow your audience are good, and sometimes they are not. Facebook is obviously the most popular channel we're all using. Facebook *business posts*, Facebook *personal posts*, and more. By the way, yes, you should be updating your Facebook page. Yes, you should be putting engaging content on there. Later, we'll discuss how you can find engaging content, but one way you should definitely be using Facebook today is by sharing *business* content on your *personal* pages, once a week—whether it be shared by you, your management, or your staff. I'm not asking you to slam people every day; I'm simply asking for you to find a valid business reason (VBR) to justify someone from your staff sharing business info on their personal Facebook page.

Suppose your restaurant has 40 employees. There's a decent chance *ALL 40* of them have a Facebook account. They all probably also have an Instagram account, a Twitter, a Snapchat account, or something they're using regularly. What you want to do is find a reason that would inspire them to help your company, the place they work, the place they want to see stay in business and thrive. Then, they can engage their friends, whether it's a contest or a special, or a Content Gathering Promotion, which we'll talk about later. This is one of the best ways for you to grow your audience: share your professional content through the personal Facebook accounts of employees, co-workers, friends, and family.

Facebook Messenger is a hugely important. *Hugely* important. **HUGELY** important! In this book, I'm going to teach you how to grow it, but first, I need to explain what it is. Facebook Messenger is email from 20 years ago—before marketers like me screwed it up. I've been doing email marketing since the early 2000's, when I started overseeing email marketing campaigns for our boat dealership. From 2000 until we got out of business in 2008, I dealt with a lot of campaigns. In those 'early' times, we saw email open rates as high as 60%, 70%, and even 80%! In short: *huge open and click-through rates* that would be considered exceptional by today's standards. But because marketers and businesses used email so much over the years, and consumers got so much of it, it simply doesn't get opened much anymore.

Email is still a valid way to do your marketing, but it's not as effective as it once was, and perhaps it never will be. And with Messenger, you're doing something you're not doing anywhere else: you're starting a conversation.

I was recently at a conference where the keynote speaker, Ryan Deiss of Digital Marketer, said something profound: "Conversations are the new lead." Isn't that true? Isn't that impactful? Where once a lead was something you could pursue or follow up with (a name, an email an address, a phone number...), NOW, it is having a conversation. Sure, you might not have their email address, or their phone number, yet, but they're having a conversation with you through Facebook Messenger. And that's what's important.

Some other big channels you might not be using (but should be) are YouTube, Facebook Live, and Facebook Videos. Did you know that restaurants sell the number one topic for videos? Yep: FOOD. In 2017, Facebook released a study that asserted the number one video topic on Facebook was food. I'm sure this trend carries over to YouTube, as well. When was the last time you walked back into your kitchen with your phone's video camera and went 'live' with your food line as someone is mixing the wings in the sauce and/or someone else is making delectable desserts? Restaurants have amazing ways to showcase their food! At times, the presentation can be downright awesome! Show people how

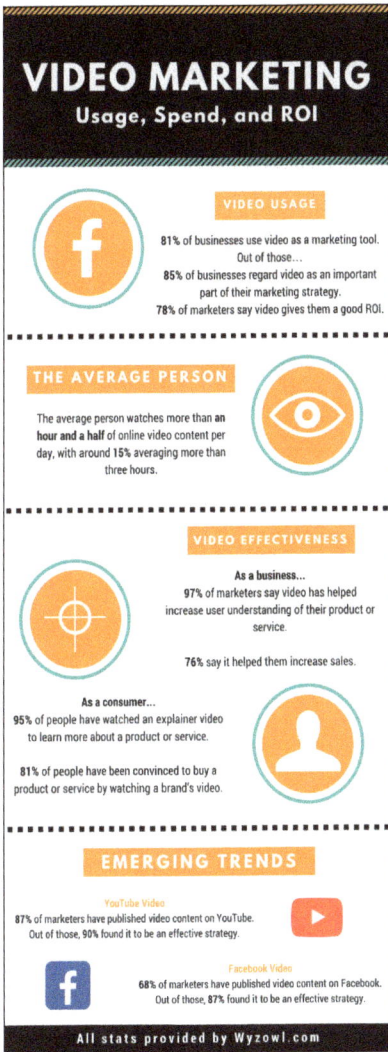

VIDEO MARKETING
Usage, Spend, and ROI

VIDEO USAGE

81% of businesses use video as a marketing tool. Out of those...
85% of businesses regard video as an important part of their marketing strategy.
78% of marketers say video gives them a good ROI.

THE AVERAGE PERSON

The average person watches more than an hour and a half of online video content per day, with around 15% averaging more than three hours.

VIDEO EFFECTIVENESS

As a business...
97% of marketers say video has helped increase user understanding of their product or service.

76% say it helped them increase sales.

As a consumer...
95% of people have watched an explainer video to learn more about a product or service.

81% of people have been convinced to buy a product or service by watching a brand's video.

EMERGING TRENDS

YouTube Video
87% of marketers have published video content on YouTube. Out of those, 90% found it to be an effective strategy.

Facebook Video
68% of marketers have published video content on Facebook. Out of those, 87% found it to be an effective strategy.

All stats provided by Wyzowl.com

you do it. I know of a German restaurant where they bring out their selection of desserts with little hearts on the pastry and they look absolutely fantastic! People LOVE seeing that kind of artistry and detail, so show it if you can.

Have you ever seen how chocolate is made? I've seen videos from certain chocolate companies or from chocolatiers, and they are fascinating. Hey, people love chocolate, so why wouldn't they love seeing how it's made? Answer: they do! Pizza is another food that people (especially kids) love seeing get made. The stretching, the tossing, the cheese and the toppings, the pizza coming out of the oven, being cut up, being pulled up with the spatula, and the gooey cheese dripping down... it's endlessly entertaining. You can even shoot it in slow motion with most phones. And if you add a tripod, or some type of stabilizer, like a gimbal, you end up with highly-sharable, professional-looking video that is smooth and not shaky.

But remember to keep your content easy-flowing and 'organic'. Customers don't want to watch video that shows pre-packaged flawlessness; they want to see what actually happens. You know, the behind the scenes stuff. So skip the video of a pizza being perfectly prepared in a perfect

˙ Video stats from the graphic are from WYZOWL.COM
Please feel free to use these statistics in any commercial or non-commercial capacity. If you use the statistics we require a reference back to Wyzowl.
https://www.wyzowl.com/video-marketing-statistics-2018/

kitchen, with a perfect chef, doing a perfect TV show, all covered by perfect video footage. That's a commercial and no one wants to watch that. They want to see something fresh and interesting. They want to see something real, or silly, or unusual. This is the new way to engage; this is the new way to talk to the people. This is what Facebook Video and especially Facebook Live can bring to your restaurant: authenticity.

Visit the link below to watch a tutorial on creating or finding amazing video content

www.roiengines.com/p/videos

Below, we'll walk you through our Top 10 ways to use Facebook Live. Of course, YouTube also has wonderful ways for you to shoot and share videos, whether it's on Facebook or on other channels.

Now for a channel that is often underused and sometimes (like email) abused: text messages. Texts, just like Facebook Messenger, can cut through the clutter. Texts don't reach the engagement level or conversational tone of Facebook Messenger, but roughly 99% of texts messages are delivered and people see them. If you have a reliable way to send out text messages, messages that are cost-effective, messages that are not spammy, messages that deliver results for your business, I think you should take advantage of the text channel.

In the next chapter, I'm going to show you how you can take these channels, create your own radio station, and then pull it all together in a systematic program that will help you grow, gather, and track your marketing. In short, we're going to show you how to create your ROI Engine.

CHAPTER 3

A System to Grow, Gather and Track: *The ROI Engine*

Now that you understand the importance of creating your own radio station, and the plethora of options available to help you do just that: Facebook, YouTube, email marketing, LinkedIn, Instagram and so on, let's turn out attention to a specific plan that will help you build that and put it all in place. We call this plan our *ROI Engine*. The ROI (Return On Investment) ENGINE is what allows you to understand what happens when you put $1, or $10, or $100 into the program. It further tells you what type of audience you're growing, and what type of sales it generates? Because, at the end of the day, if you're not measuring and tracking what you're doing in marketing, you're losing.

Let's examine the four elements of the ROI Engine. The first element is *GROW*. The second element is *DRIVE*. The third element is *REDEEM*. And the fourth element is *TRACK*.

GROW. We're going to help you create your radio station using Facebook and Instagram ads, along with Facebook's Audience Network, all of which are available through Facebook's Ads Manager platform. We're going to help put the right ads in front of the right audience to build awareness for your restaurant. Also, we'll get a better sense of your past (and future!) clientele, and learn whose information you will need to grow a new and better database, without duplication or redundancy with what you already have.

There are some exciting things to keep in mind as we go forward with this plan. The first is scalability. Facebook's ad platform allows you to determine your precise budget. You can increase or decrease your budget as your business fluctuates. Perhaps you start to see quick success and want to go from $500 to $750 or from $750 to $1000 per month. The ROI Engine allows you to understand what happens every time you add a dollar and how that might 'generate back'. It allows you to accurately predict how many people will be added to your database, and how many people will be driven into your restaurant that month if you increase the budget by a hundred dollars.

WARNING. This isn't a get-rich-quick scheme; we're building an audience over the course of a year. This isn't an idea that you put in place and, in 60 short days, your restaurant has quadrupled its influx of cash at the register. That's possible, but not likely to happen. This is a plan that'll help you consistently grow your database over the course of six to twelve months. I believe you'll start to see things really cook about six months into the process, thanks to the size of the database you can now reach out to on a consistent basis, every month.

DRIVE. When you build an audience that you control, you're *driving traffic*. For this job, I recommend you use Facebook Messenger and email marketing. As I've already noted, Messenger is where email was 20 years ago. We are literally seeing open rates of 80%, 90%, and sometimes even 100%! I know that sounds crazy, but it's true. That's what we are seeing and so are a lot of businesses all over the internet. And the click-through rates are almost as impressive, with rates of 40%, 50%, and 60%. Translation: this is a unique and powerful medium you can use to communicate with your customers and potential customers. Naturally, we will eventually be gathering email addresses, because, at the end of the day, email still works. Used correctly, it can definitely help you drive business.

When we talk about driving business, please keep in mind that we're not talking about herding cattle (or cats). You'll be controlling the who, the when, and the why of it all. You'll be driving exactly those people into your restaurant *WHOM* you desire... *WHEN* you desire them... and *WHY* you desire them. This isn't a promotion where, every month like clockwork, you send a free appetizer promotion or a *buy-one-get-one-free* coupon. We don't want you to condition your audience or your followers to believe that every thirty days, they'll be confronted with an email that's as boring and predictable as that. I know many restaurants (too many!) that run the same, lame coupons in the same, lame coupon magazines month after month after month. But guess what? Research shows that most of the people who redeem these types of coupons would be coming in, already, so all these restaurants did was give a bunch of their regular customers a discount for no good business reason.

Mind you, there's nothing wrong with offering your customers something that has real value, it's just that the devil is in the details. Yes, you want to give them something awesome and desirable because—let's face it—you're trying to bribe them into giving you their information. You're trying to get them into your restaurant family, and people aren't going to join your 'family' for a $5 off coupon. So let's consider a different approach, such as: *Win a Year's Worth of Free Burgers!* Consumers love an offer like this, because it sounds quite valuable. But the value is more *perception* than *reality*, for while this may sound huge on the front end of the equation, when you study an offer like this closely, it doesn't cost the restaurant a thing! In fact, it actually makes the restaurant money, because the winner will likely be bringing a friend or family member in with them, and that friend is going to be spending money. But this is exactly the kind of promotion people will flock to. They *will* come to your restaurant to register for something of this nature. And for you, it's the perfect *have-your-cake-and-eat-it-too* offer; it brings new people in without giving them discount.

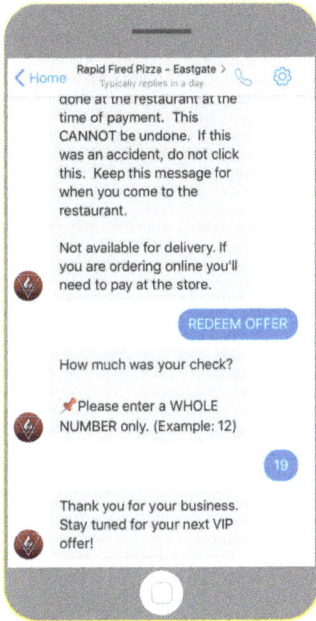

REDEEM. This is the lynch-pin to the entire program. Why? Because if you don't know *who* is walking in, and *when* they're walking in, and *what* they're walking in for, and *how much* they're spending per visit to your restaurant, then you can't create a predictable program. The redeemable element has a lot of unique aspects to it. First, it allows you to control what you are offering, because the offers are 'removable'. Once a customer comes in uses their phone to redeem a digital 'coupon', the offer is no longer available to them. Since it has been used, it disappears from their phone. The old way of doing things is completely uncontrollable. Upon viewing a post or an email, a customer would be instructed to "show this offer to your server to redeem your coupon". But once redeemed, it still existed on their phone. In theory, a customer could come in and redeem the offer every day of the week for seven days straight. And the work-arounds of a quick expiration date or a hyper-specific offer only serve to depress your redemption rates. By having a redeemable product that can be controlled, you don't have to worry about that, because a customer comes in, redeems the offer, and it goes away.

Another interesting element to our way of offering redeemables is that it allows you to be selective; you can *exclude* people from partici-pating in the future. Imagine that your tripwire for people registering for your program is a free appetizer. But why offer a free appetizer to the folks who have already registered in the past? By having a *redeemable of-fer*, you'll know exactly who's in the program, and who's been a redeemer in the past. Once you know who they are, you can exclude them from seeing your tripwire in the future. They will only see your other (new to them) marketing efforts; they won't see the same promotion over and over as they do with the aforementioned monthly coupon magazine of-fer. In summary, imagine if coupon magazines could somehow be pro-grammed to bypass those houses that had already redeemed the coupon in months gone by. How powerful would that be?!? Well, guess what? That is precisely the kind of results this program can deliver to you!

Redeemable offers also let you optimize your campaigns for the future. Suppose that during a three-month period, you get 600 people to walk into your restaurant and redeem one of your of-fers. Of that 600, let's say 400 are strong custom-ers whose spending habits are solid, 100 are average customers, and 100 are terrible. Facebook can help you create what they call *Custom Audi-ences*—a digital marketing approach that allows you to load your data, and then target appropriate people, accordingly.

In this way, your 400 ideal, big-spending, awesome customers can become the foundation of an incredible Custom Audience in Facebook. And, as if that wasn't already fantastic enough, you can even create a 'look-alike' audience based off of that original audience. In short, Face-book can seek out and find for you people who 'look' just like those good people you already LOVE having in your restaurant. With the tens of thousands of targeting elements that Facebook has developed, they have the ability to find people on a granular level that's simply unbelievable. Think how that would feel—*knowing* your ads are going to your perfect, potential customer.

TRACK. This is where things get really juicy: the trackable side of all this data. Every month, you'll be able to look back and analyze your programs and understand what they did, and why. Of course, you're still *Growing* your list and you're still *Driving* your customers in, particularly in the first month, which we refer to as the opt-in month. And each month after that first one, as people opt in, they get different, targeted promotions. Maybe it's a lunch offer, maybe it's a dinner offer, maybe it's a special Sunday offer, maybe it's a contest promotion for only that month. Regardless, you'll have two things to track. First, you'll follow the people who opt in each month, and follow how many offers they redeemed, and how much they spent. Second, you'll follow the people who were *already in the program* from prior months, who then came in for the monthly offer, and you can follow how much they spent when they came in.

Every month, you'll be able to look back and see your program grow, because you're spending isn't likely to change much every month. Let's say you gather an average of 500 people per month. And say you spent roughly $500 to attract those folks though your Facebook Ads. Well, in the second month, you spend $500 to get 500 new people, BUT you've still got your original 500 paying attention to you, so now you're effectively having a conversation with 1,000 people. Flash forward to the tenth month and, though you're spending $500 to get 500 additional people, in reality, you've collected 5,000 people into your database that you can now talk to through Messenger and email marketing!

That is how this program can really start to grow and hum along. With the ability to track so accurately, you can look back and understand precisely how the different offers presented each month helped or hurt the program. And, further, how different customers interacted with the program. And, ultimately, how you can continue to hone and optimize the program. But perhaps most importantly, you can see the direct correlation between the money you spend — and the money that spending generates in revenue. In essence, you'll learn how much is it costing you every time somebody walks in through your doors. For example, if your

$100 spend drives 40 customers into the restaurant who, in turn, spend various amounts of money, you'll be able to calculate your per customer acquisition cost. Understanding your acquisition cost, and understanding your maintenance cost is critical.

In the meantime, don't be worried if you're new to Facebook Ads, Facebook Messenger, or email marketing. We're going to help you. Every chapter is going to have step-by-step instructions, and there will be links that will take you to *How-To* videos, and PDFs that allow you to chart your progress and mark off the steps as you go.

Are you starting to feel overwhelmed? Do you want to get RIGHT TO THE TRAINING? Visit the link below to find to check out our online training site where we WALK YOU THROUGH exactly how to build this and introduce you to a community of restaurant owners and marketers who can help you.

www.roiengines.com/p/jointoday

CHAPTER 4

Why Use Offers That Are Redeemable and Not "Show This"

A marketing ploy that I see used often (and poorly) by a lot of restaurants is the "Show this offer to redeem" approach. It's especially popular on Facebook, Instagram, and Twitter. The concept is fine; it's the execution that's lousy. Yes, the restaurant computer can track those five offers that got redeemed, leading to $100 in revenue. But, they have no way to track *who* redeemed them, or *how* much they spent. Nor can they create follow-up or *sequence-marketing* on those people.

By my count, there are five MAJOR problems with this approach:

PROBLEM ONE: you will lean toward putting a short expiration date on the offer. If you've got a 30-day window on an offer that states, "Show this to your server for a free appetizer", a customer can come in 10, 20, 30 times in the next month. As a result, you're essentially forced to put a narrow time frame on the offer. "Show this in the next five days." "Show this is the next three days." "Show this TODAY!" What's the upswing? In my opinion, not much. Or even less than not much. My research[1] has shown that the shorter the window, the smaller number of redemptions you're going to get. By shrinking the time frame of an offer, you've just eliminated a large portion of your crowd, who, for whatever reason, can't come in during the window of opportunity.

PROBLEM TWO: you'll have no method for excluding people who have already redeemed the offer. By asking for someone to "*show this*" you are obviously not operating in a cutting-edge arena. Things that are "shown" can't get measured, or registered, or become data-points. There is no way

---

[1] Just to be clear, I've done this kind of work for seven crazy-wonderful years, with *hundreds* of restaurants, *hundreds of thousands* of offers, *tens of thousands* of offers redeemed, in all types of restaurants, bar and grills, and breweries.

of knowing that someone used it. However, if you use an offer that has a redeemable feature baked-in, like we do, you can exclude a customer from seeing that offer in the future. A good example is something we experienced recently. One of our clients had a large percentage of folks who had never redeemed an offer from three, four, or five months ago. We emailed those people — and only those people — who had *not redeemed* that old offer. In essence, we gave them another chance to check out our client's restaurant while simultaneously helping them improve quarterly sales. And it worked, and guess what, there wasn't a cost to sending this message.

PROBLEM THREE: you can't optimize your campaigns. As already noted, when you do a *"show this"* offer, you do not gather the slightest bit of data. Alternatively, with a redeemable offer, the sky's the limit. A good example is our client, Rapid Fired Pizza. From a pool of about 1,400 recent opt-ins, they've seen 150 offers redeemed in just the past week! And when they redeem the offer, we are able to constantly update the Custom Audience in Facebook and, by extension, the 'lookalike' audience as well. Think about that. You're optimizing your campaign based on what you think the ideal customer looks like. How great is that?! We all should have been doing that from the start. And even better, you can optimize the campaign based on those people who are opting in.

PROBLEM FOUR: you can't exclude customers who don't spend enough. Say you've got 500 people over a two-month period who redeem your offer. And of those 500 people, 400 of them spend the ideal average ticket (or higher), and 100 don't. Well, with our program, you can create Custom Audiences based on those variables. You can say, "Hey Facebook, here's 100 people who spent $5. I don't want those low-spenders coming back. I want the happy folk who spend $35." You can create exclusion audiences — Custom Audiences — around those people, and then create lookalike audiences by saying, "Hey Facebook, here are 500, fun, happy people who spent a lot of money in my joint. Find me 500 more who look just like that!"

PROBLEM FIVE: you can't measure your ROI. It's hard to understand your ROI when the variables aren't all known. And without some of the necessary data, it's like measuring for drapes without a measuring stick.

With our program, we've got it all. We have those desirable metrics. We know who everybody is and what they're like. We know where every penny has been and what it's done along the way. We know everyone's email address and how we can optimize all this information for the future, so we can get a crystal-clear understanding of our ROI.

What do I mean? Imagine you got 1,000 opt-ins, but only 50 redemptions. That's not good. In fact, that's pretty sucky. But what does it mean? It means you're targeting the wrong people. If, on the other hand, your 1,000 opt-ins nets 300 redemptions, then you know you're looking at a much stronger ROI. And a deeper understanding of the campaign's ROI. But with a "show this" campaign, you'd be sitting in the dark. Without our program, you wouldn't know a darn thing about the ROI of your marketing efforts. So, PLEASE, drop all the nonsense and start using OUR program for YOUR restaurant. You'll go stronger, farther, deeper, and get much better results. What's more, you'll understand your marketing spend so well that in the future, every dollar you spend will deliver ten times the results you're seeing today.

CHAPTER 5

Software We Use

We use specific software with this ROI Engine program. Hey, don't worry; we're not going to overwhelm you. We'll show you how to get the exact training you need at every step, so you can easily create this amazing program for your restaurant.

First and foremost, we use Facebook Ads. Facebook Ads drive people to respond to the 'call to action' that we create. You'll also need Facebook Ads Manager, which you might already have if you have a Facebook business page. If so, it's just a matter of activating it. You'll see a link on this page to further your understanding of how to do that.

Visit the link below to find out more about the Facebook Business Manager
www.roiengines.com/p/businessmanager

The next software you'll need is ManyChat. While you could use a similar Facebook Messenger/chat-bot program, I recommend ManyChat for the simple reason that all of our tutorials reference ManyChat and the sequences we're going to have you build and get access to are on ManyChat. That, plus I think it's the best tool for the job. ManyChat is a program that allows you to hook Facebook up to an automation sequence. As you see to the right, when somebody comments on your post or engages in your content, they get a messenger sequence asks for their information and then presents them with their first offer, we also use Messenger Scan Codes for this as well.

The next software you'll need is a product called Zapier. To help illustrate what Zapier does, imagine you're driving on the expressway that runs near you home. However, the exit ramp that used to get you to your house no longer exists, so you can't get to your house. You've got to find another way... Well, Zapier is a product that helps you connect things that are, otherwise, disconnected. For example, software. While Facebook and ManyChat are integrated with each other, they are not connected to Google Sheets. Zapier can make that connection happen.

Speaking of Google Sheets, that's the next software we employ in our program. It's basically Microsoft Excel online (on Google). With Google Sheets, we can store the data that flows from our marketing efforts. In this way, everybody who interacts with the Facebook post, or goes into Facebook Messenger with ManyChat, gets routed through Zapier over to Google Sheets. We thus get their first name, last name, email address, Facebook ID, the offer they have access to, how much they spend, and so on. That valuable data can then be stored there, online. From there, we can pull it over to other places, like a point-of-sale program or a customer management program.

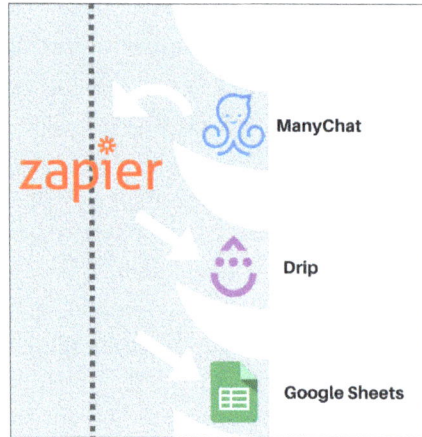

Finally, we use an email automator, called Drip (see the link, below, to sign up for a free trial). Drip allows you to do things that traditional email can't do. With Drip, we can build a sequence of emails that people will get, gradually, from the moment they opt in. A week after they opt in, they get a reminder notice pertaining to the offer. A couple of weeks after that, they get another notice about the offer. And, most importantly, Drip allows us to take people OUT OF THAT EMAIL SEQUENCE, so if they have redeemed the offer, they no longer get reminder notices.

To recap, Facebook Ads Manager, ManyChat, Google Sheets, Zapier, and Drip are the products you're going to need to build your program. Feel free to go ahead and check out the reference guide in this chapter to find links to free trials to some of those programs.

Visit the link below to get access to all of the software you'll need to run the ROI Engine

www.roiengines.com/p/software

CHAPTER 6

Offers – Opt-in Offer & Future Traffic-Driving Promos

Before we get to building the ROI Engine for your restaurant, we've got to tackle a very, very important subject: your opt-in offers. And, beyond that, your plan for future offers.

As I've already suggested, your opt-in offer is like a bribe you pay to your customers in order to get their valuable information. The more convincing your offer, the more likely you'll get results: *more info* from *more people*. In a nutshell, to get information from your customers or your future customers, you're going to have to present them with something that TRULY APPEALS TO THEM.

Joe's Brewhaus　•••

How would you like 10% OFF you next meal?
Show this post to your server to get 10% your meal!

👍 Like　　💬 Comment　　↪ Share

That is different for different types of restaurants. One example might be a restaurant that takes in an average check of $10, usually from people coming in solo. Or maybe they come in with coworkers for lunch. If you give away a free sandwich, these folks aren't likely going to have a big overspend; they're going to get a drink and a side, and the restaurant will net a couple bucks. If, on the other hand, we consider a quick turnover, sit-down restaurant, where the average check is about $35 — a free appetizer offer is still likely to net checks on the order of $30 to $40, because these patrons will almost certainly order two entrees and some drinks.

For obvious reasons, it is important to be aware of these differences, but, ultimately, the key point to focus on is that coupons will never inspire customers to volunteer their information; they can get a coupon in any magazine, without giving up a drop of data. No, they want something exclusive — and they want to know the potential exists for them to get something exclusive in the future.

I once had a client a client who objected to the idea of doing a no-strings-attached, free appetizer. He much preferred connecting the free appetizer to the purchase of an entrée. So I suggested we do a split test: we would test both offers, with two different audiences, at three different restaurants, to see which one did better. Well, after a few months of testing, the data came back. For every 100 customers who walked in to

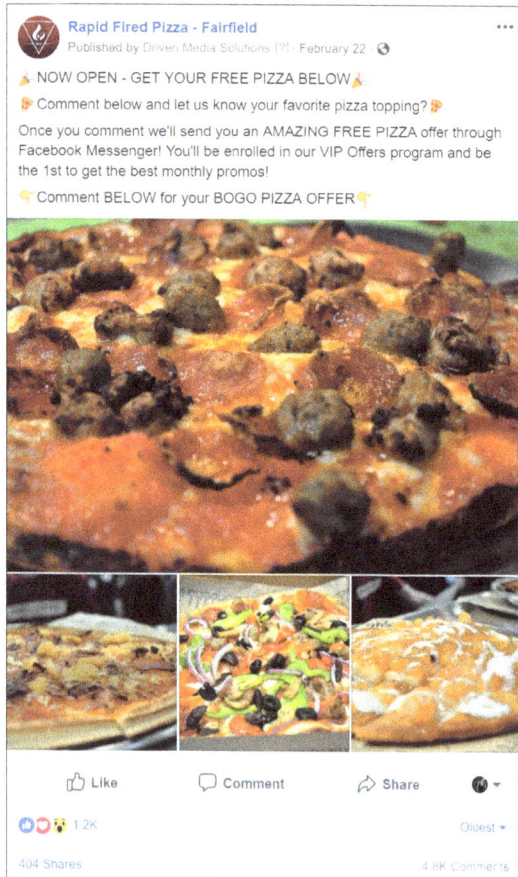

Rapid Fired Pizza - Fairfield
Published by Driven Media Solutions [?] · February 22

NOW OPEN - GET YOUR FREE PIZZA BELOW
Comment below and let us know your favorite pizza topping?
Once you comment we'll send you an AMAZING FREE PIZZA offer through Facebook Messenger! You'll be enrolled in our VIP Offers program and be the 1st to get the best monthly promos!
Comment BELOW for your BOGO PIZZA OFFER

Like   Comment   Share

1.2K   404 Shares   4.8K Comments

redeem the free appetizer with the purchase of an entrée, *130* walked in and redeemed the free appetizer with no strings attached. But even more significant, with the no-strings-attached offer, the average ticket was $11 more per customer.

Here's the simple but compelling math: in the first scenario, we attracted 100 people, who each spent roughly $40; in the second scenario, we attracted 130, who each spent roughly $51. Which customers do *you* want? I know, it's an easy question to answer. I also know some of you might be asking, "But what about those people who came in and spent no additional money?" Yes, there were some of those types. We found that 5% to 8% of the people would order their free appetizer, and spend less than $8, Generally speaking, these were the regular locals who would drop in to hang out at the bar. But 5 to 10 people buying a beer or an extra appetizer is a small price to pay to bring in 130 people spending $11 more than average. So you've got to look at the positive side, not the negative. And the positive is, they gain a couple thousand dollars in revenue, just check out the chart below.

If you run a fast-food restaurant, you're probably not going to get that level of overspend; you'll have a lot of people on the front end redeeming their free offer before simply moving on. In this case, you've got to evaluate your best *beginning* opportunity, and then evaluate how you can work to move them down a different path in the future.

For example, we work with a pizza restaurant that is, for all intents and purposes, a fast-food place. People typically come solo or as a couple. Occasionally, a family drops in. And so, we didn't start off with a no-strings-attached, free pizza; we started off with a buy-one-get-one-free offer, which was a fresh concept that had a little buzz to it. Because it was digital, meaning it wasn't a lame coupon splashed across every local newspaper or magazine, the buy-one-get-one-free offer worked great. The long and the short of it is that every situation is going to be a little bit different.

I *have* been involved with fast-food restaurants that have done very well with a free sandwich offer, but the key is in recognizing that the offer's main goal was to get people into the database and, soon thereafter, into the restaurant.

The future offers are where you need to be focusing on getting them back, because a restaurant that's a fast-food restaurant over a sit-down restaurant, is going to get people back more often. At the fast/casual restaurants we typically see in our program, people come once or twice every month. With fast-food, we see them every week. And so, yes, you have a lower ticket, but you have a higher quantity. So when you're looking at your future offers, you need to be planning these out in advance.

I've put a chart and a spreadsheet online for you to study and download. It will give you some guidance as to how you might want to think about your offers. For example, do you want to settle for a few awesome offers per year — or do you want to create offers that will drive business during those run-of-the-mill days you don't typically have strong traffic? Your rent, electric, and utilities don't change day to day, so why not drive some revenue toward your Mondays, Tuesdays or Wednesdays, when sales are relatively weak? You might never make your Mondays perform exactly like your Saturdays, but you will drive some cash flow to make your month look and feel better, and that's precisely what these offers can do: drive sales to time periods when you otherwise wouldn't have them, but can afford to offer *more, bigger*, and *better* incentives.

And please don't forget: your offer doesn't always need to incorporate a discount. I've already mentioned how I'm not a fan of programming customers into thinking they're going to get a discount from you, every month. Contests do the job better *and* are more exciting. People truly seem to enjoy the uniqueness of contests. Opportunities to "Win a $500 Gift Card!" or "Register to Win Your Very Own March Madness Party!" or "Enter to Win Free Lunch for a Year!' are sure-fire ways to bring customers to your establishment; customers who will not only be happy to pay full-price, but will also be happy to give you their all-important and valuable data!

Just think of all the possibilities! With that in mind, we've put an exciting PDF online for you to examine and download. In it, you'll find a host of ideas you can consider plugging in to your own program. *PLUS,* you'll get a glimpse of the month-by-month strategies we've employed to create new and future customers.

Visit the link below to find out WHY offers vs coupons
www.roiengines.com/p/offers

CHAPTER 7

Diving into the ROI Engine—
What Is It Going to Do?
(A detailed walk through...)

ROI ENGINE

Okay, I've teased you enough. Let's turn our attention to the actual ROI Engine. In the next few chapters, we're going to breakdown the key processes and guide you to specific URLs that will teach you how to accomplish all we've touched on. In the final analysis, these processes aren't easily comprehended by simply reading about them. However, by watching short videos, you can literally build the program as you follow along.

We're going to run highly-targeted Facebook Ads aimed at people who 'look just like' your best customers, people who should and will be your customers, people who are your customers but haven't been loyal, and people who are your customers but aren't currently visible to you because they aren't on your email list. We're going to show you how to upload your current databases, eliminate folks you *don't* want while including folks you *do* want. And, if you don't have a database, we're going to help you create one from scratch.

We usually refer to our ads as *call-to-action* or *engagement* ads, because they pose important questions to our patrons. If you look at the ads on the right, you'll see examples of this approach. What we're trying to do with our ads is encourage meaningful engagement. For example: "What is your favorite appetizer to order when you go out to eat? Add your comment, below, and we'll send you an outstanding VIP Offer through Facebook Messenger.

Not only will this trigger the Facebook Messenger automation sequence we've talked about, it's going to give you rich content for your down-the-road marketing. To the right, you can see examples of

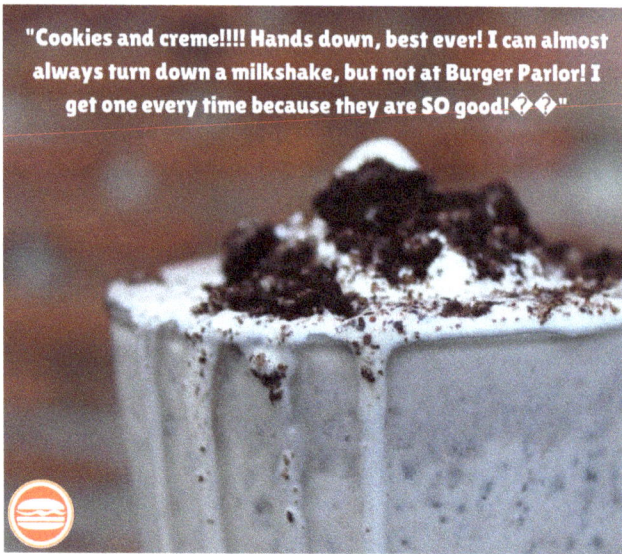

"Cookies and creme!!!! Hands down, best ever! I can almost always turn down a milkshake, but not at Burger Parlor! I get one every time because they are SO good!��"

engagement we generated for Burger Parlor. Some of the descriptions people are sharing with us regarding their dining preferences and the food they enjoy are incredibly detailed. Imagine how you could use comments such as these to create graphics for your restaurant or for your restaurant's online profile.

Once people comment, it's going to trigger an automated sequence in Facebook Messenger using ManyChat: "Great. What is your email address so we can proceed?" Once they input their email address, that automatically triggers an offer being sent out through email *and* Facebook Messenger. And further, that customer has now been added into our permanent direct-email database through Zapier and Google sheets. Lastly, we can add them onto our ManyChat and Messenger subscriptions.

What follows is pretty awesome. When the customer walks into the restaurant and redeems the offer, they immediately get a thank you message, which acts as a kind of 'carrot' — inspiring them to come back into the restaurant for future offers. At the same time, we capture what they spent, when they spent it, what they spent it on, all of which obviously helps with future marketing efforts.

This customer behavior also automatically triggers REMINDERS that will be sent out in the future. These reminders let people know they if haven't redeemed their offer yet: "Hello, Janice, did you know you've still got a free appetizer waiting for you at Escargot Café? Make sure you come in and redeem it, soon!" When people *do* redeem it, we take them out of the reminder sequence and they're instantly bumped to the list for next month's offer.

So now you know what the program does, and you have a basic understanding of how it works. NOTE: It is important to know that there are certain rules and restrictions you will need to follow when working within Facebook's Messenger platform, but we'll get to the details of that later.

Let's See It In Action
www.roiengines.com/p/roiengine

CHAPTER 8

Facebook Ads

Before you create your own Facebook ad, there are a few things you'll want to consider. The first is determining and understanding the audiences that you're going to target. The second is the type, style, and tone of the ad you'll want to create. And the third is the ad copy.

The type of audiences you create are going to vary based on your customer data. For starters, you could create an audience based around those people who have engaged with your Facebook business page or your content in the recent past. I like to cap this at around 60-90 days, because if you go any further back, you're going to get people who have moved out of the area or who aren't coming to your restaurant anymore.

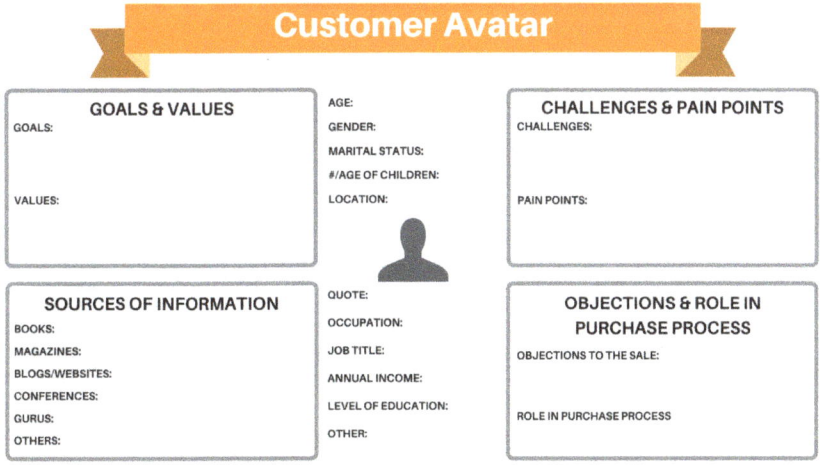

Customer Avatar

GOALS & VALUES
GOALS:

VALUES:

AGE:
GENDER:
MARITAL STATUS:
#/AGE OF CHILDREN:
LOCATION:

CHALLENGES & PAIN POINTS
CHALLENGES:

PAIN POINTS:

SOURCES OF INFORMATION
BOOKS:
MAGAZINES:
BLOGS/WEBSITES:
CONFERENCES:
GURUS:
OTHERS:

QUOTE:
OCCUPATION:
JOB TITLE:
ANNUAL INCOME:
LEVEL OF EDUCATION:
OTHER:

OBJECTIONS & ROLE IN PURCHASE PROCESS
OBJECTIONS TO THE SALE:

ROLE IN PURCHASE PROCESS

The next step is to look at the *different types* of page engagement. For example, if you have videos on your Facebook business page, that is a terrific audience to target. Suppose you've posted twenty videos in the past six months. Your Custom Audience can be based on the specific folks who engaged with those videos. But mere engagement isn't enough; you'll want to target those who have actually watched a good portion of the videos — say at least 25% of the video's length. In other words, if one of your videos is a minute long, this audience would have watched it for 15 seconds or more. Choose as many videos as you think you need for this purpose (I suggest going back in time about three months), and then create your audience out of those people who have engaged with 25% of those videos.

The next Custom Audience will flow out of your customer database because, with Facebook Ads, you can include or exclude people based on whether or not they are in a certain type of audience. Let's assume you have a large email database. We're going to take that list and load those people into the program and we're going to create a new Custom Audience that we'll call your *Restaurant Email Database*. Now we can create a 'lookalike' audience based on the features, attributes, and characteristics of that first audience. Facebook enables you to take that list, choose the country you're operating in, and create a new Custom Audience based off of people who 'look just like' the people currently in your database. Needless to say, when you create your ads, you're going to choose the zip codes and the cities that can help narrow the broad selection down to just your local area, because the last thing you want to do is run an ad that reaches far and wide when you know that nobody's likely to drive more than five miles to get to your restaurant.

The second aspect of your customers that you can target is whether or not they have recently eaten at your establishment. For example, if your email database ties in with a loyalty program that tells you exactly which people have been in during the past 30 days (and which have not), which people have been in during the past 60 days (and which have

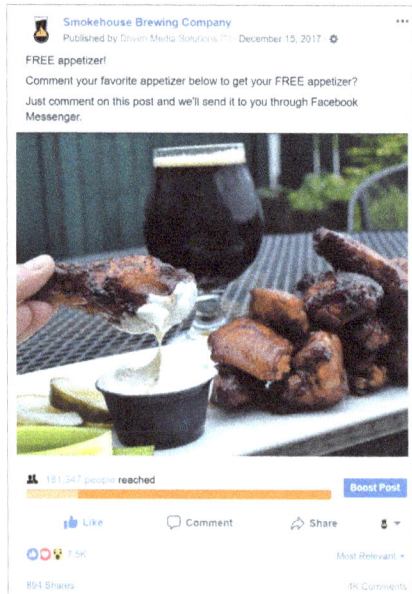

Smokehouse Brewing Company
Published by Driven Media Solutions [?] · December 15, 2017 ·

FREE appetizer!
Comment your favorite appetizer below to get your FREE appetizer? Just comment on this post and we'll send it to you through Facebook Messenger.

181,347 people reached   Boost Post

👍 Like   💬 Comment   ↪ Share

😊👍❤ 7.5K   Most Relevant ▾

854 Shares   1K Comments

not), which people have been in during the past 90 days (and which have not). You can use that data to create different Custom Audiences, such as "Recent Customers 30 Days, Exclude" or "Customers Who Have Not Been In in 60 days, Include". Those are just a couple of examples of how you could name these target audiences. Later, we'll steer you to a video will explain how and why you use these audiences to grow your business.

As to the question of *what type of ad* you create, there are a lot of different options. In our program, we primarily use *engagement ads* because what we're doing is creating engagement with your Facebook business wall. To get some organic reaction, these ads can be open to anybody to start off with, which I recommend. Or, they can be shared as an unpublished (or dark) post, which would be hidden from your wall. There are pros and cons to both, but they share the exact same goal: inspiring people to comment on the post.

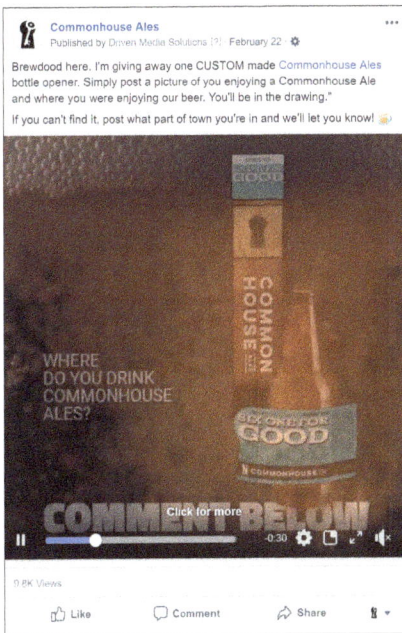

You can use either videos or pictures in this type of post. The problem that I typically encounter with using videos is that you'll be required to pay when people watch that video, even when that's done by accident, on their newsfeed. Obviously, this will drive up your acquisition cost. Pictures don't present you with this 'accidental view' problem, because they are simply not engaged in the same way a video is. If you use a video, you're paying for engagement with the video, and engagement with a video is defined by how many people watch it. Engagement with a picture is different. Your ad's ad copy will inspire people to comment, liked, or share a post, but that behavior doesn't trigger the same engagement costs.

The last but most important part you'll need to focus on and create is the actual ad. We'll share some examples of ads that have performed well for us, but ultimately, it all comes down to a few key questions you must ask yourself: How are you planning to engage/interact with your customer? Exactly what are you offering them? And lastly, what is your call to action? (I.e. What is the *direction* you are giving to them? What's their next step?) Boiling all this down, you've got to be able to say: Here is *what* we're going to give you. Here is *how* we're going to give it to you. Here is *why*. And here is *where*.

It could even be something as simple as this: "Tell us what your favorite appetizer is and we'll send you an amazing offer through Facebook Messenger!" You can set the stage in so many ways, but an important, final element of your ad is the graphic or photo you will use. It's got to be awesome (and, oh boy, it *definitely* can't be weak!) You can get your pictures or graphics from many sources, but, by far, THE BEST SOURCE is user-generated.

Before moving on to the next chapter, please explore the additional references we've provided, then go online, and learn more about why some ads work better than others.

Visit the link below to find out more about Facebook Custom Audiences
www.roiengines.com/p/customaudiences

CHAPTER 9

Messenger & ManyChat

Now we're ready to dive into Facebook Messenger, one of the most important elements of the ROI Engine. At the risk of beating a dead horse (forgive me, but it is THAT IMPORTANT for you to understand!), I'll again reiterate that Messenger is email, circa 1998, when people were actually excited to open up anything and everything. They were fascinated to see what was coming to them through this brand-new medium. Well guess what? — Facebook Messenger is today's brand-new medium! So much so that a familiar, tongue-in-cheek saying in our business suggests that *we marketing-types haven't had a chance to ruin it yet!* Translation: for the next year or two, Facebook Messenger is going to be off the hook! You *WILL* get 80 to 90% open rates! You *WILL* get 40 to 60% click-through rates! You *WILL* inspire amazing engagement! But beyond all that, Messenger is unlike any other marketing program we've ever experienced, because it allows us to engage in conversations with our present and future customers. To grossly understate the significance of this, I'll just point out that conversations like these are rather unusual in the marketing world.

Now let's turn our attention to ManyChat, Messenger's important ally and sidekick. ManyChat is an automation program that allows you to incorporate sequences, or 'bots', into your marketing *through* Messenger. We're going to use ManyChat for three main functions: First, we'll use ManyChat as a comment growth tool, similar to some of those we've already referenced. People comment on your post and thereby engage with it, which triggers an automation sequence in Messenger. Second, we'll use ManyChat's REFURL, which is simply another way to place somebody into that automation sequence in Messenger. Typically, you're using REFURLs to drive activity on landing pages, on your website, on emails, and even in-house advertising via Scan Codes. In this way, you'll be able to market to people as they're leaving your restaurant (or soon after) — giving them a chance to opt in to the program you've created in Messenger. Third, we'll use ManyChat's broadcast feature, which is another way to share offers with your customers and expose them to your monthly communication. From month to month, that communication can vary — from a contest to a discount to a special promotion or even a simple ad. With messenger, the possibilities are practically endless.

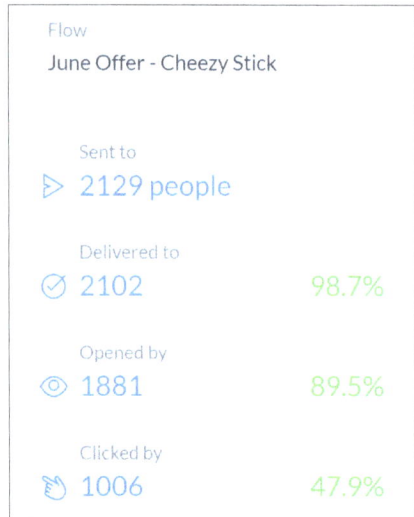

Flow
June Offer - Cheezy Stick

Sent to
▷ 2129 people

Delivered to
⊘ 2102   98.7%

Opened by
👁 1881   89.5%

Clicked by
👆 1006   47.9%

Visit the link below for an overview on Facebook Messenger Automation
www.roiengines.com/p/messenger

CHAPTER 10

Zapier

As previously noted, Zapier is an *integration software* that allows us to tie multiple platforms together, and get the information you've gathered from ManyChat and Facebook into other powerful programs. Zapier is amazing, but it is probably the most intimidating product we use in the entire sequence, because so many people are unfamiliar with it. However, Zapier becomes much more comprehensible when you remember the expressway ramp analogy that I shared earlier. If you can envision a world without ramps allowing you to get ON or OFF the highway, Zapier steps in to fill that role. Zapier is the connector ramp.

It works like this: when people comment on your Facebook business post, they'll be using Facebook Messenger. This, in turn, will take them through a series of questions that will motivate them to opt in to the subscription and share their email address. At that point, you will deliver your offer to them. The minute they give you the email address in Many-Chat, they will be 'tagged' in a specific way. We typically use the tag of 'VIP Offer' or perhaps that month's subscription offer. We call the tasks that Zapier performs 'zaps' and here is when a 'zap' will be triggered: when a new person is tagged and it pulls the data from Messenger and moves it where you want or need it.

In our case, we'll be moving that data to Google Sheets. We're also pushing it to the email program, Drip, because we'll be enrolling those people who just opted in. The next thing we'll use Zapier for is updating the Google Sheet with the person's usage of your program, and to temporarily take them out of the email campaign, if necessary.

Let me give you an example. Suppose a customer opts in on May 1st. The minute they opt in, they're added to the Google Sheet. Now you know you have a subscriber in ManyChat and in Drip. And, because they're enrolled in the campaign from that zap in Drip, they get an

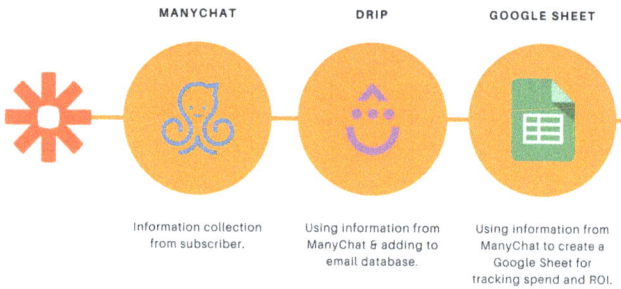

MANYCHAT	DRIP	GOOGLE SHEET
Information collection from subscriber.	Using information from ManyChat & adding to email database.	Using information from ManyChat to create a Google Sheet for tracking spend and ROI.

email offer. But then, say, May 7th comes around and they haven't redeemed the offer, yet. Well, since we have them in Google Sheets and we've already activated the automation setups, by May 8th, they're going to get an email in Drip reminding them of their VIP Offer they've yet to claim.

Let's continue to suppose that, on May 9th, they come into your restaurant and redeem their offer through Messenger. They enter the dollar amount they spent, which triggers a second zap, which tells the Google Sheet the exact amount that customer spent, along with the data signaling that that particular offer was redeemed. At that moment, ManyChat & Drip temporarily takes this customer out of the email & Messenger sequence by changing their 'tag'. This process keeps customers from receiving any future automation reminders, but *much more importantly*, it has fed you the data you need to monitor your program.

Every time we spend money to acquire opt-ins, we should want to know: ONE: how many opt-ins were generated; TWO: how many patrons came in; and THREE: how much money did they each spend. With a combination of our Google Sheet and our Cyfe dashboard, we can do just that. This set-up allows us to see how much people *spent*, what their *average check* was, how many of them *came in* and, more importantly, how much we spent to acquire all that.

In this way, we can continuously analyze the marketing program to see how we can improve it, if necessary, or, if it's already going great, how we maintain that success.

Visit the link below for an overview on Zapier
www.roiengines.com/p/zapier

CHAPTER 11
Google Sheets

Google Sheets is basically an online version of Microsoft Excel. It allows us to easily store the data of every customer who comes through our marketing funnel. Also, it reports on how customers use the program. We create a sheet that has a tab for every different aspect of the program: the number of opt-ins per month, the number of redemptions per month, the number of transactions per month, and the amount of sales per month. Then, of course, we have a tab for each *month*, a tab for each *customer* in the program, and a tab for *customer behavior*. One of the main purposes of Google Sheets is to store the customer data so that we can reference it in future steps. Through Zapier, we can go into Google Sheets and pull up information that will help us communicate with customers. It's a great place to store this data, and *all of the information* we gather through the program. Please click on the link, below, to check out an actual Google Sheet for yourself.

Have you joined the ROI Engine yet?

www.roiengines.com/p/jointoday

CHAPTER 12
Drip Email

Drip email is what we recommend you use for this program for numerous reasons. First, it's an email program that is meant to facilitate automation. There are a lot of email programs out there that we use for our clients (Constant Contact, Mail Chimp, etc.) that are good for doing service emails on a monthly basis. But they're not specifically built with automation in mind.

Think of Drip in this way: If you pull a tree out of the ground and turn it upside-down, you can take a water hose and drench the trunk of that tree. Soon enough, water is going to travel down the trunk and spread out across a lot of different branches. That's kind of what Drip gives you the ability to do. When someone 'enters' into an automation sequence — depending on how they interact with your marketing — they will get a variety of different emails. If a customer hasn't redeemed an offer, you would want them to get an email reminder. If a customer has redeemed an offer, you would want to send them a thank-you note. Simply put, there are a lot of things you can do in Drip.

Showing **Campaign** Emails								
	Opens	Clicks	Unsubscribes	Status	Delay Between Emails			
Here's Your 1st VIP Offer From Rapid Fired Pizza ▷	56.6%	0.0%	0.2%	Published	Immediately			Edit ▾
Don't Forget About Your BOGO Craft Pizza ▷	41.3%	0.0%	0.2%	Published	8 days		⚙	Edit ▾
Come See Us & Use Your VIP Offer	31.9%	0.0%	0.1%	Published	12 days		⚙	Edit ▾

The other reason we use Drip is that it has the ability to update your Custom Audiences in Facebook. The reason that is important is that it will help optimize your ads. The Facebook algorithm will 'look' to see who's opting in to your ads, and they will optimize them to find more people like that, while costing you less money.

The number one way to optimize your ads is based on *conversions*. Every time somebody redeems an offer in the ROI Engine, it goes through Google Sheets, and, from there, to Drip, where a Custom Audience gets created. And then it's updated in Facebook with the people who have opted in, as well as the people who actually spent money.

Drip Automation Workflow

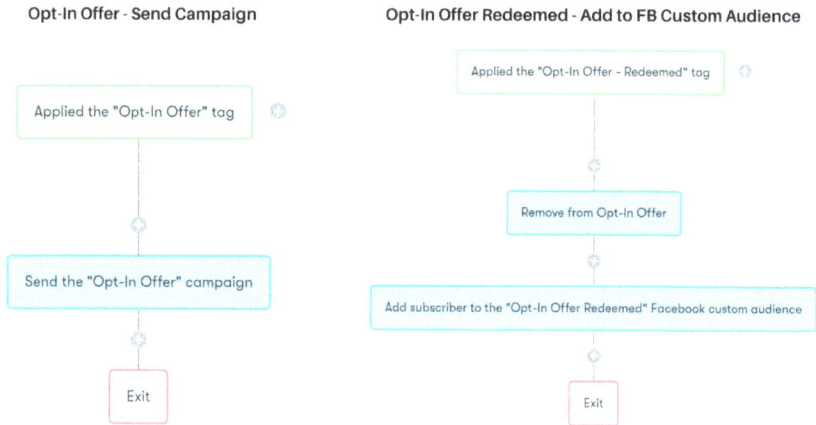

Opt-In Offer - Send Campaign

Applied the "Opt-In Offer" tag

Send the "Opt-In Offer" campaign

Exit

Opt-In Offer Redeemed - Add to FB Custom Audience

Applied the "Opt-In Offer - Redeemed" tag

Remove from Opt-In Offer

Add subscriber to the "Opt-In Offer Redeemed" Facebook custom audience

Exit

Some more advanced features of Drip can include an understanding of how much people spend in comparison to others, and then placing them in to particular audiences depending upon that information. Let's say the average check in your restaurant is $40 and someone comes in and redeems an offer for under $15. That is not particularly desirable. However, if another customer comes in and spends $40, $50, or $60, that *IS* desirable. Through Drip and Facebook, you can make distinctions and create Custom Audiences based on their spending habits. For example, you could create an 'exclusion' audience for people who spend $20 or less. And, of course, based on those people who reliably spend $50 to $70, you could create an 'inclusion' audience, and then a 'look-alike' audience, which will help make your ads more impactful, down the road, and, in so doing, give you a better chance for long-term success.

Visit the link below for a Drip Email tutorial.
www.roiengines.com/p/drip

CHAPTER 13
Testing Your Program

Now that you have built your ROI Engine, it's time to test your program. We'll do this before we build your offer or your ad. You're simply 'running' the engine to make sure everything is working properly. This is something you should have more than one account for, not to mention a few friends to whom you can send links to test things out.

As always, we'll share some online videos online, but please bear some things in mind: When using the comment growth tool, if you have already commented on the particular post you're testing with, then you can't do it again; it will recognize you and it won't fire the automation in Facebook Messenger. To avoid the hassle of having to create new posts, you can go back a month or two on your business page, and find a post that is insignificant — i.e. one that nobody commented on. Since there's no reason it will generate any action now, hook up your comment growth tool to that post.

But I do strongly recommend having one or two other Facebook profile accounts that you can use for testing. I have friends and staff accounts that I test-use pretty consistently. In this way, I can simultaneously have a couple windows open on my computer and, using an incognito window in Google Chrome, I'll have my main Facebook account hooked up, with Many Chat, etc. all 'live' and another window on the second screen. That way, I can 'comment' on the post and go through the entire sequence to see if it functions properly.

You're going to want to test, test, test — *A LOT*, because you DO NOT want this going live if it is not going to work right. After you have everything figured out and it's firing correctly, shoot a link of your post to three or four friends, and have them test-drive it so they can let you know what they think. Was it easy? Was it smooth? Did it go through?

Speaking of testing, if you're a member of our online program, you'll be able to test-post your ads to a private Facebook group that we will set up for just that purpose. This will allow you to get feedback from real people in the community and let them test it, as well.

CHAPTER 14

Your Offer & Ad

Okay, now it's time to talk about your ad and your offer. To repeat: You've got to think of this as if you are bribing the consumer for their information and, typically, you can't bribe somebody with a coupon.

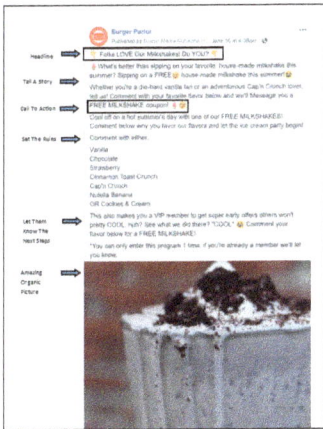

From a restaurant's perspective, there are two ways to look at this. If you're a restaurant with an average ticket of $10-15, you're more than likely going to take more of a hit up front, since you're going to have people get your offer and come in without delivering a huge overspend. On the other hand, there will be a bigger upside as things progress. After all, consumers eat at a casual dining restaurant about once a week (maybe every *other* week), but they eat fast-food two or three times a week. In the final analysis, the value is in getting them on your list so that you can entice them to come back two or three times a month to your restaurant. Plus, you didn't even have their contact info before, or a way to communicate with them through Messenger, so that's all icing on the cake.

At the casual dining restaurant, you're going to have a bigger win up front, because your free no-strings-attached appetizer will bring in more people who, in turn, will spend $30-40 each. So you'll have a larger win in those early months, but that will be offset by the fact that people don't eat at your restaurant as often as with fast-food restaurants. At the end of the day, both concepts are bringing in valuable data for use down the road. You've just got to realize that the pay-off is *earlier* with higher ticket restaurants, and *later* with lower ticket restaurants.

But regardless of the kind of establishment you run, one bit of the advice I give never changes: *do not give offers that suck!* Do not give lousy coupons on an opt-in. Do not give offers that are available someplace else, like $10 or $25 off your bill. You want to create an exclusive, VIP offer, so please do that!

When it comes to your future offers, feel free to change things up a bit; work on bringing them at different parts of the day, or driving them in with one-of-a-kind contests. One option is to mix up the offers every month — four months in a row — and then repeat. We've linked to some pages that take you to our online guides that share ideas as to how you might structure your offers.

Now for the ad. Your ad has to be memorable; it has to grab their attention. But it also has to stay within Facebook's guidelines, so don't go overboard. Use a picture in your opt-in ad, maybe one you change up every few months to keep things fresh. And alter the frequency with which you make your changes, too. You want to appeal to different audiences, so don't be stale. And don't forget that different foods appeal to different people.

Also remember that we favor pictures over videos, because so often customers will never see that video get launched onto their timeline as it automatically starts up. It might run for 5, 10, 15 seconds before they even notice its playing and close it up without ever engaging with it. But, if it played long enough, you just got charged for an 'engagement' that never really happened.

When it comes to pictures, such as in an ad that asks folks to comment on their favorite pizza topping or tell us what their favorite appetizer, you will get charged when they comment, like, or share, but that's the kind of engagement that pays dividends. So, that's why we lean towards pictures versus videos.

Now, with regards to the ad copy, you need to abide by Facebook's terms of service. Facebook's terms of service are simple. Since they are giving you access to *their customers*, they want your data in return. Truthfully, it's more complex than that, but when you boil it down, that's the underlying reality. If you can provide Facebook with more data on their customers, they will be happier and, in the long run, you will be happier, too.

Another thing you should be aware of is that you should not be running ads that don't lead to real interaction. Ads that say type, "Win below!" or "Free below!" don't stimulate meaningful engagement; in those instances, Facebook does not gain any valuable data. But if you're ad inspires a longer, more in-depth response, this helps Facebook 'grow' the data on those users. Examples of questions that might stir longer engagement could be: "When was the last time you were at the restaurant?" or "What is your favorite appetizer?" or "Have you ever been to our restaurant before? If you answered 'yes', what meal did you enjoy?" "Of all the ice-creams we offer, what is your favorite?" Questions like this encourage more engagement and give you, and Facebook, richer data.

You also want to set the terms of what you plan on doing next. In some cases, we let people know, in advance, that if they comment on their favorite appetizer, we will send them a message through Facebook Messenger that tells them they will get an exclusive offer when they subscribe to our VIP Offers Program. In this case, you're essentially setting the table. You're letting them know what their actions will gain them. That's a really important element to keep in mind.

Visit the link below to get a VERY clear understanding of why you need to have AWESOME offers for your program!

www.roiengines.com/p/awesomeoffers

CHAPTER 15
Other Marketing Elements

Now let's consider some other, non-advertising ways, to drive traffic into this program. One of the easiest methods to achieve this is an 'organic' post on some or all of your social media channels. While this approach is intended for people who are currently fans of your company, it can also net responses from individuals who are merely on your email subscription list. Not infrequently, the latter group will opt in as a result. The larger point is that, if you don't already have a Facebook Messenger subscription from them, you might, in this way, easily gain another touch point. You can post on Facebook, share through community groups, share on Twitter, share on Instagram, share on LinkedIn, share with your friends, and then ask people to return to your Facebook page to comment on the original post. If you have a YouTube channel add a REFURL at the end of the video description with a call to action. Your employees can share it on their personal timeline(s) and drive people there, as well. When it comes to driving organic traffic, this is the lowest hanging fruit available to you.

Next is email. (Remember email?!) I'm guessing you've got a sizable email database. I'm also guessing you've got a lot of people in that database who have forgotten about you and, perhaps, vice versa. They have not visited your establishment in some time and need a reason to get excited about coming in. But though you have their email, you don't have their subscription in Messenger. To remedy this, you can create a *ref URL* in the growth tools of Many Chat. When people click on that link, it will take them into Messenger and place/subscribe them into the sequence. In summary, by simply using your current email list, and with no

JOIN OUR VIP OFFERS PROGRAM

JOIN TODAY & START GETTING EXCLUSIVE OFFERS & PROMOS! VISIT THE LINK BELOW TO GET STARTED

VIPOFFERS.LIVE/GUTHRIESCHICKENFAIRFIELD

additional cost to you, you're going to be able to grow your Messenger Program and your VIP Offers Program.

You can also use the ref URL on your website and for in-store campaigns. Below, you'll see some banners we created for the website, along with some other simple digital elements we have circulating. We also have business cards that we hand out at the register, where the host or cashier simply asks your customer, "Hey, are you a member of our VIP offers program? If not, go to this URL or scan this code and opt in to get your free appetizer or your free sandwich." What better way to get the people into this program who already know, like, and trust you? And as a bonus, there is no acquisition cost because you acquired them, yourself. That in turn will drive down the cost of the entire program and make your ROI even better.

Visit the link below to find out ways to drive FREE traffic into your program.
www.roiengines.com/p/organic

CHAPTER 16

Training Staff

Training your staff to understand, buy-in, and execute your program is critically important. Indeed, this piece commonly gets overlooked with regard to marketing initiatives. I know, because I have been guilty of overlooking this factor, myself. In the not too distant past, I developed a promotion for a company that was incredibly successful. Like, gangbusters, off-the-hook successful. So successful, in fact, that it almost failed! Good thing this was a business I'm a partner in.

The campaign kicked off about 8:00 pm on a Sunday night. By about 9:30 the same night, 2 of our staff had already received 15 to 20 text messages about 'free sessions' — and they were absolutely clueless as to what this all meant. When they called me, I told them what was going on, but also confessed I had no idea this program would be picking up speed so fast. In the end, we got through it, but I learned my lesson right then and there: Training your staff to understand, gain buy-in, and execute your program is critically important, which is why I'm so adamantly preaching this lesson to you, now. We've actually created a client onboarding page with short videos on every step of the program for our clients to give to their staff. On this webpage we cover the program, possible issues and how to treat the customers.

Beyond keeping your staff abreast of all campaigns and specials, they must understand that *any offer* a customer brings through the door should be treated like cash, or even *better* than cash! After all, there's a good chance that offer means a customer is visiting for the very first time, so they should be treated like royalty. The staff needs to be trained to understand that these customers are no different than a customer who comes in with a wad of $100 bills. Make sure everyone takes extra special care of these folks, because we want to bring them back over and over and over again. That is how you grow your database and a growing database almost always correlates to money in the bank.

Now the next part is pretty simple: you need your staff to understand all the little ins-and-outs of the entire program. They need to know why it is in place, what it looks like, how it will interact with your customers, how to redeem offers for your customers, how they will operate the program, and how they will operate *within* the program. You will also want to teach them about any possible problems or sticking points that could come up. Once you've followed all the online tutorials and understand how to build your program, you will need to create your own restaurant-specific video(s) that you can forward to your staff. This video(s) will be a permanent reference point if your staff ever needs to brush up and refresh their memories.

Finally, I recommend you create laminated flyers, like you will see when you follow the link, below. This flyer will give your staff a step-by-step walk-through of all we've been discussing. In this way, you will reduce the chance for surprises, since your staff will be up-to-speed and well-educated, which in turn will lead to happier and more loyal customers.

The link below will take you to a page we created to help our clients understand the program and to help them train their staff.

www.roiengines.com/p/clienthelp

CHAPTER 17

Tracking & Analysis

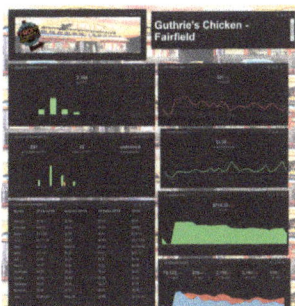

One of the greatest features of this entire program is that it is *trackable*. You're able to monitor the entire, interconnected process through Messenger and Google Sheets. As you begin to build it, you will see how easily your program will create data reports in Google Sheets, and how you can tie that back to an online dashboard that will show you what's happening — moment-by-moment, day-by-day, week-by-week, and month-by-month. Keep in mind, you've got to flex your brain and analyze these numbers to be sure the program is giving you what you need. Also, analyzing the numbers will help you highlight which customers you should be *adding to* — or *excluding from* — your various Facebook Custom Audiences based on their spending traits. Below we've linked to a video that goes through the dashboard we've created and what we monitor. Understanding your results will keep you up to speed on how you can use Custom Audiences to optimize your campaign to ENGAGE more people in the profile you do want (heavy spenders), but EXCLUDE more people in the profile you don't want (light spenders). You have the ability to see the amount you've spent on the offers that have been redeemed, and then determine if that's a good expenditure or bad expenditure. Once you get used to it, the tracking is really simple. Use Google Sheets to pay attention to what's being reported through the entire program and make sure you're using that data to drive the program ahead in the future.

See the link from the last chapter to watch a video on the Cyfe Dashboard

CHAPTER 18
YOU DID IT!

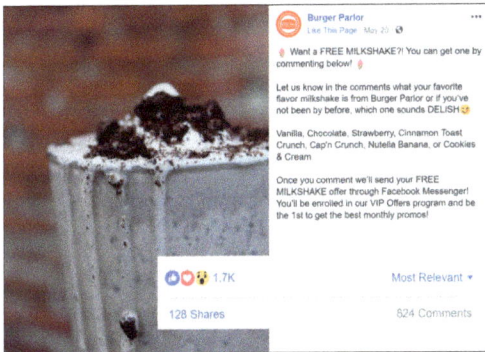

Congratulations, you did it! I'm hopeful that by this point, you have rolled up your sleeves, taken the initiative, and wandered into the online tutorials and have built out your very own ROI Engine. If so, you are far ahead of the vast majority of your competitors, nationwide, and should be reaping the benefits any day. If not, and you have just read this book for the first time, cover to cover, beginning to end, then you are now ready to go back through to explore the tutorials. Please be sure to first join our Facebook community to take advantage of the wide and wonderful variety of free resources we have given you. Let us know if you've any questions.

I'm so glad you came along for this book journey and I'm excited about how we can help you grow your own *radio station* and drive trackable results through Facebook advertising. This big, bold step will undoubtedly help you develop a more successful and sustainable business.

I appreciate the time you've taken to invest in your marketing almost as much as you *will* appreciate the time you've taken to invest in your marketing!

GOOD LUCK!

Have you joined the ROI Engine yet?
www.roiengines.com/p/jointoday

About the Author I've been in marketing since 1998 and I've seen it all. My career started on 2 paths at the same time. First I started in Radio Advertising sales in 1999 and then in the Fall of 1999 I bought a book on how to create an Adobe Pagemill website for a business my father, brother and myself decided to start, a Boat & RV Dealer. Building that site was the first time I EVER did anything on the internet. We eventually grew the dealership to be one of the largest in the region and we were selling MANY units every month online through our website, chat rooms and email marketing. The steam didn't pick up though until 2004 when I stumbled upon the power of online marketing directly to consumers through discussion boards in forums about their passion, like boating and camping. It was here that I learned about SEO and started diving into digital marketing. In 2008 I founded Driven Media Solutions, a digital advertising agency with a big focus on Facebook. This was years before most businesses would realize that Facebook and other Social Media platforms were places they needed to be.

My experience on all sides of the equation is what's helped with grow my business. I'm not only worked in advertising selling it, and as an agency helping plan and place it, but as the client. Our boat dealership allowed me to understand the pain of buying advertising that either did not work or that you didn't know worked. When I started Driven Media Solutions in 2008 it was to help businesses get online and understand if what we were doing was working or not. Then in 2015 it was National Pretzel Day (a great Hallmark restaurant holiday) that showed me the path. We had been doing marketing for restaurants for 4 years with a decent amount of success, but it wasn't until this day that I saw the potential of Facebook for restaurants. A $150 spend on 3 ads yielded $18,000 in sales for 3 restaurants. From there it took off and that was the force behind creating the ROI Engine.

www.ingramcontent.com/pod-product-compliance
Lightning Source LLC
Chambersburg PA
CBHW041733200326
41518CB00019B/2580